I0158007

The Poetry of Bliss Carman

Volume V - Ballads of Lost Haven

A Book of the Sea

William Bliss Carman was born in Fredericton, in New Brunswick on April 15th 1861. He was educated at Fredericton Collegiate School before moving to the University of New Brunswick, obtaining his B.A. there in 1881. As is common with so many writers his first published piece was for the University magazine and for Carman that was in 1879.

After several years editing various magazines and periodicals Carman first published a poetry volume in 1893 with Low Tide on Grand Pré. There was no Canadian company prepared to publish and when an American company did so it went bankrupt.

The following year was decidedly better. His partnership with the American poet Richard Hovey had given birth to Songs of Vagabondia. It was an immediate success.

That success prompted the Boston firm, Stone & Kimball, to reissue Low Tide on Grand Pré and to hire Carman as the editor of its literary journal, The Chapbook.

Carman brought out, in 1895, Behind the Arras, a somewhat more serious and philosophical work centered on the premise of a long meditation, using the speaker's house and its many rooms, as a symbol of life and the choices to be made.

In 1896 Carman met Mrs Mary Perry King, who rapidly became patron, adviser and sometime lover. She also became his writing collaborator on two verse dramas.

In 1897 Carman published Ballad of Lost Haven, and in 1898, By the Aurelian Wall, the title poem itself was an elegy to John Keats and the book was a collection of formal elegies.

As the century turned Carman was hard at work on a five-volume set of poetry "Pans Pipes". The excellence of a number of these poems did much to install Carman as the most noted of Canadian Poets and eventually their own Poet Laureate.

In 1912 the final work in the Vagabondia series was published. Richard Hovey had died in 1900 and so this last work was purely Carman's. It has a distinct elegiac tone as if remembering the past works themselves.

On October 28th, 1921 Carman was honored by the newly-formed Canadian Authors' Association where he was crowned Canada's Poet Laureate with a wreath of maple leaves.

William Bliss Carman died of a brain hemorrhage at the age of 68 in New Canaan on the 8th June, 1929.

Index of Contents

A SON OF THE SEA

I was born for deep-sea faring;
I was bred to put to sea;
Stories of my father's daring
Filled me at my mother's knee.

I was sired among the surges;
I was cubbed beside the foam;
All my heart is in its verges,
And the sea wind is my home.

All my boyhood, from far vernal
Bourns of being, came to me
Dream-like, plangent, and eternal
Memories of the plunging sea.

THE GRAVEDIGGER

Oh, the shambling sea is a sexton old,
And well his work is done.
With an equal grave for lord and knave,
He buries them every one.

Then hoy and rip, with a rolling hip,

He makes for the nearest shore;
And God, who sent him a thousand ship,
Will send him a thousand more;
But some he'll save for a bleaching grave,
And shoulder them in to shore,—
Shoulder them in, shoulder them in,
Shoulder them in to shore.

Oh, the ships of Greece and the ships of Tyre
Went out, and where are they?
In the port they made, they are delayed
With the ships of yesterday.

He followed the ships of England far,
As the ships of long ago;
And the ships of France they led him a dance,
But he laid them all arow.

Oh, a loafing, idle lubber to him
Is the sexton of the town;
For sure and swift, with a guiding lift,
He shovels the dead men down.

But though he delves so fierce and grim,
His honest graves are wide,
As well they know who sleep below
The dredge of the deepest tide.

Oh, he works with a rollicking stave at lip,
And loud is the chorus skirled;
With the burly rote of his rumbling throat
He batters it down the world.

He learned it once in his father's house,
Where the ballads of eld were sung;
And merry enough is the burden rough,
But no man knows the tongue.

Oh, fair, they say, was his bride to see,
And wilful she must have been,
That she could bide at his gruesome side
When the first red dawn came in.

And sweet, they say, is her kiss to those
She greets to his border home;
And softer than sleep her hand's first sweep
That beckons, and they come.

Oh, crooked is he, but strong enough
To handle the tallest mast;
From the royal barque to the slaver dark,
He buries them all at last.

Then hoy and rip, with a rolling hip,
He makes for the nearest shore;
And God, who sent him a thousand ship,
Will send him a thousand more;
But some he'll save for a bleaching grave,
And shoulder them in to shore,—
Shoulder them in, shoulder them in,
Shoulder them in to shore.

THE YULE GUEST

And Yanna by the yule log
Sat in the empty hall,
And watched the goblin firelight
Caper upon the wall:

The goblins of the hearthstone,
Who teach the wind to sing,
Who dance the frozen yule away
And usher back the spring;

The goblins of the Northland,
Who teach the gulls to scream,
Who dance the autumn into dust,
The ages into dream.

Like the tall corn was Yanna,
Bending and smooth and fair,—
His Yanna of the sea-gray eyes
And harvest-yellow hair.

Child of the low-voiced people
Who dwell among the hills,
She had the lonely calm and poise
Of life that waits and wills.

Only to-night a little
With grave regard she smiled,
Remembering the morn she woke
And ceased to be a child.

Outside, the ghostly rampikes,
Those armies of the moon,
Stood while the ranks of stars drew on
To that more spacious noon,—

While over them in silence
Waved on the dusk afar
The gold flags of the Northern light
Streaming with ancient war.

And when below the headland
The riders of the foam
Up from the misty border rode
The wild gray horses home,

And woke the wintry mountains
With thunder on the shore,
Out of the night there came a weird
And cried at Yanna's door.

"O Yanna, Adrianna,
They buried me away
In the blue fathoms of the deep,
Beyond the outer bay.

"But in the yule, O Yanna,
Up from the round dim sea
And reeling dungeons of the fog,
I am come back to thee!"

The wind slept in the forest,
The moon was white and high,
Only the shifting snow awoke
To hear the yule guest cry.

"O Yanna, Yanna, Yanna,
Be quick and let me in!
For bitter is the trackless way
And far that I have been!"

Then Yanna by the yule log
Starts from her dream to hear
A voice that bids her brooding heart
Shudder with joy and fear.

The wind is up a moment
And whistles at the eaves,
And in his troubled iron dream

The ocean moans and heaves.

She trembles at the door-lock
That he is come again,
And frees the wooden bolt for one
No barrier could detain.

"O Garvin, bonny Garvin,
So late, so late you come!"
The yule log crumbles down and throws
Strange figures on the gloom;

But in the moonlight pouring
Through the half-open door
Stands the gray guest of yule and casts
No shadow on the floor.

The change that is upon him
She knows not in her haste;
About him her strong arms with glad
Impetuous tears are laced.

She's led him to the fireside,
And set the wide oak chair,
And with her warm hands brushed away
The sea-rime from his hair.

"O Garvin, I have waited,—
Have watched the red sun sink,
And clouds of sail come flocking in
Over the world's gray brink,

"With stories of encounter
On plank and mast and spar;
But never the brave barque I launched
And waved across the bar.

"How come you so unsignalled,
When I have watched so well?
Where rides the Adrianna
With my name on boat and bell?"

"O Yanna, golden Yanna,
The Adrianna lies
With the sea dredging through her ports,
The white sand through her eyes.

"And strange unearthly creatures

Make marvel of her hull,
Where far below the gulfs of storm
There is eternal lull.

"O Yanna, Adrianna,
This midnight I am here,
Because one night of all my life
At yule tide of the year,

"With the stars white in heaven,
And peace upon the sea,
With all my world in your white arms
You gave yourself to me.

"For that one night, my Yanna,
Within the dying year,
Was it not well to love, and now
Can it be well to fear?"

"O Garvin, there is heartache
In tales that are half told;
But ah, thy cheek is pale to-night,
And thy poor hands are cold!

"Tell me the course, the voyage,
The ports, and the new stars;
Did the long rollers make green surf
On the white reefs and bars?"

"O Yanna, Adrianna,
Though easily I found
The set of those uncharted tides
In seas no line could sound,

"And made without a pilot
The port without a light,
No log keeps tally of the knots
That I have sailed to-night.

"It fell about mid-April;
The Trades were holding free;
We drove her till the scuppers hissed
And buried in the lee.

"O Yanna, Adrianna,
Loose hands and let me go!
The night grows red along the East,
And in the shifting snow

"I hear my shipmates calling,
Sent out to search for me
In the pale lands beneath the moon
Along the troubling sea."

"O Garvin, bonny Garvin,
What is the booming sound
Of canvas, and the piping shrill,
As when a ship comes round?"

"It is the shadow boatswain
Piping his hands to bend
The looming sails on giant yards
Aboard the Nomansfriend.

"She sails for Sunken Harbor
And ports of yester year;
The tern are shrilling in the lift,
The low wind-gates are clear.

"O Yanna, Adrianna,
The little while is done.
Thou wilt behold the brightening sea
Freshen before the sun,

"And many a morning redden
The dark hill slopes of pine;
But I must sail hull-down to-night
Below the gray sea-line.

"I shall not hear the snowbirds
Their morning litany,
For when the dawn comes over dale
I must put out to sea."

"O Garvin, bonny Garvin,
To have thee as I will,
I would that never more on earth
The dawn came over hill."

Then on the snowy pillow,
Her hair about her face,
He laid her in the quiet room,
And wiped away all trace

Of tears from the poor eyelids
That were so sad for him,

And soothed her into sleep at last
As the great stars grew dim.

Tender as April twilight
He sang, and the song grew
Vague as the dreams which roam about
This world of dust and dew:

"O Yanna, Adrianna,
Dear Love, look forth to sea
And all year long until the yule,
Dear Heart, keep watch for me!

"O Yanna, Adrianna,
I hear the calling sea,
And the folk telling tales among
The hills where I would be.

"O Yanna, Adrianna,
Over the hills of sea
The wind calls and the morning comes,
And I must forth from thee.

"But Yanna, Adrianna,
Keep watch above the sea;
And when the weary time is o'er,
Dear Life, come back to me!"

"O Garvin, bonny Garvin—"
She murmurs in her dream,
And smiles a moment in her sleep
To hear the white gulls scream.

Then with the storm foreboding
Far in the dim gray South,
He kissed her not upon the cheek
Nor on the burning mouth,

But once above the forehead
Before he turned away;
And ere the morning light stole in,
That golden lock was gray.

"O Yanna, Adrianna—"
The wind moans to the sea;
And down the sluices of the dawn
A shadow drifts alee.

THE MARRING OF MALYN

I

THE MERRYMAKERS

Among the wintry mountains beside the Northern sea
There is a merrymaking, as old as old can be.

Over the river reaches, over the wastes of snow,
Halting at every doorway, the white drifts come and go.

They scour upon the open, and mass along the wood,
The burliest invaders that ever man withstood.

With swoop and whirl and scurry, these riders of the drift
Will mount and wheel and column, and pass into the lift.

All night upon the marshes you hear their tread go by,
And all night long the streamers are dancing on the sky.

Their light in Malyn's chamber is pale upon the floor,
And Malyn of the mountains is theirs for evermore.

She fancies them a people in saffron and in green,
Dancing for her. For Malyn is only seventeen.

Out there beyond her window, from frosty deep to deep,
Her heart is dancing with them until she falls asleep.

Then all night long through heaven, with stately to and fro,
To music of no measure, the gorgeous dancers go.

The stars are great and splendid, beryl and gold and blue,
And there are dreams for Malyn that never will come true.

Yet for one golden Yule-tide their royal guest is she,
Among the wintry mountains beside the Northern sea.

II

A SAILOR'S WEDDING

There is a Norland laddie who sails the round sea-rim,
And Malyn of the mountains is all the world to him.

The Master of the Snowflake, bound upward from the line,
He smothers her with canvas along the crumbling brine.
He crowds her till she buries and shudders from his hand,
For in the angry sunset the watch has sighted land;
And he will brook no gainsay who goes to meet his bride.
But their will is the wind's will who traffic on the tide.
Make home, my bonny schooner! The sun goes down to light
The gusty crimson wind-halls against the wedding night.

She gathers up the distance, and grows and veers and swings,
Like any homing swallow with nightfall in her wings.
The wind's white sources glimmer with shining gusts of rain;
And in the Ardise country the spring comes back again.
It is the brooding April, haunted and sad and dear,
When vanished things return not with the returning year.
Only, when evening purples the light in Malyn's dale,
With sound of brooks and robins, by many a hidden trail,
With stir of lulling rivers along the forest floor,
The dream-folk of the gloaming come back to Malyn's door.
The dusk is long and gracious, and far up in the sky
You hear the chimney-swallows twitter and scurry by.
The hyacinths are lonesome and white in Malyn's room;
And out at sea the Snowflake is driving through the gloom.
The whitecaps froth and freshen; in squadrons of white surge
They thunder on to ruin, and smoke along the verge.
The lift is black above them, the sea is mirk below,
And down the world's wide border they perish as they go.
They comb and seethe and founder, they mount and glimmer and flee,
Amid the awful sobbing and quailing of the sea.
They sheet the flying schooner in foam from stem to stern,
Till every yard of canvas is drenched from clew to ear'n'.
And where they move uneasy, chill is the light and pale;
They are the Skipper's daughters, who dance before the gale.
They revel with the Snowflake, and down the close of day
Among the boisterous dancers she holds her dancing way;
And then the dark has kindled the harbor light alee,
With stars and wind and sea-room upon the gurly sea.
The storm gets up to windward to heave and clang and brawl;
The dancers of the open begin to moan and call.
A lure is in their dancing, a weird is in their song;
The snow-white Skipper's daughters are stronger than the strong.
They love the Norland sailor who dares the rough sea play;
Their arms are white and splendid to beckon him away.
They promise him, for kisses a moment at their lips,
To make before the morning the port of missing ships,
Where men put in for shelter, and dreams put forth again,
And the great sea-winds follow the journey of the rain.
A bridal with no morrow, no welling of old tears,

For him, and no more tidings of the departed years!
For there of old were fashioned the chambers cool and dim,
In the eternal silence below the twilight's rim.
The borders of that country are slumberous and wide;
And they are well who marry the fondlers of the tide.
Within their arms immortal, no mortal fear can be;
But Malyn of the mountains is fairer than the sea.
And so the scudding Snowflake flies with the wind astern,
And through the boding twilight are blown the shrilling tern.
The light is on the headland, the harbor gate is wide;
But rolling in with ruin the fog is on the tide.
Fate like a muffled steersman sails with that Norland gloom;
The Snowflake in the offing is neck and neck with doom.
Ha, ha, my saucy cruiser, crowd up your helm and run!
There'll be a merrymaking to-morrow in the sun.
A cloud of straining canvas, a roar of breaking foam,
The Snowflake and the sea-drift are racing in for home.
Her heart is dancing shoreward, but silently and pale
The swift relentless phantom is hungering on her trail.
They scour and fly together, until across the roar
He signals for a pilot—and Death puts out from shore.
A moment Malyn's window is gleaming in the lee,
And then—the ghost of wreckage upon the iron sea.

Ah, Malyn, lay your forehead upon your folded arm,
And hear the grim marauder shake out the reefs of storm!
Loud laughs the surly Skipper to feel the fog drive in,
Because a blue-eyed sailor shall wed his kith and kin,
And the red dawn discover a rover spent for breath
Among the merrymakers who fondle him to death.
And all the snowy sisters are dancing wild and grand,
For him whose broken beauty shall slacken to their hand.
They wanton in their triumph, and skirl at Malyn's plight;
Lift up their hands in chorus, and thunder to the night.
The gulls are driven inland; but on the dancing tide
The master of the Snowflake is taken to his bride.

And there when daybreak yellows along the far sea-plain,
The fresh and buoyant morning comes down the wind again.
The world is glad of April, the gulls are wild with glee,
And Malyn on the headland alone looks out to sea.
Once more that gray Shipmaster smiles, for the night is done,
And all his snow-white daughters are dancing in the sun.

III

THE LIGHT ON THE MARSH

The year grows on to harvest, the tawny lilies burn
Along the marsh, and hillward the roads are sweet with fern.
All day the windless heaven pavilions the sea-blue,
Then twilight comes and drenches the sultry dells with dew.
The lone white star of evening comes out among the hills,
And in the darkling forest begin the whip-poor-wills.
The fireflies that wander, the hawks that flit and scream,
And all the wilding vagrants of summer dusk and dream,
Have all their will, and reck not of any after thing,
Inheriting no sorrow and no foreshadowing.
The wind forgets to whisper, the pines forget to moan,
And Malyn of the mountains is there among her own.
Malyn, whom grief nor wonder can trouble nevermore,
Since that spring night the Snowflake was wrecked beside her door,
And strange her cry went seaward once, and her soul thereon
With the vast lonely sea-winds, a wanderer, was gone.
But she, that patient beauty which is her body fair,
Endures on earth still lovely, untenanted of care.
The folk down at the harbor pity from day to day;
With a "God save you, Malyn!" they bid her on her way.
She smiles, poor feckless Malyn, the knowing smile of those
Whom the too sudden vision God sometimes may disclose
Of his wild, lurid world-wreck, has blinded with its sheen.
Then, with a fond insistence, pathetic and serene,
They pass among their fellows for lost minds none can save,
Bent on their single business, and marvel why men rave.
Now far away a sighing comes from the buried reef,
As though the sea were mourning above an ancient grief.
For once the restless Mother of all the weary lands
Went down to him in beauty, with trouble in her hands,
And gave to him forever all memory to keep,
But to her wayward children oblivion and sleep,
That no immortal burden might plague one living thing,
But death should sweetly visit us vagabonds of spring.
And so his heart forever goes inland with the tide,
Searching with many voices among the marshes wide.
Under the quiet starlight, up through the stirring reeds,
With whispering and lamenting it rises and recedes.
All night the lapsing rivers croon to their shingly bars
The wizardries that mingle the sea-wind and the stars.
And all night long wherever the moving waters gleam,
The little hills hearken, hearken, the great hills hear and dream.
And Malyn keeps the marshes all the sweet summer night,
Alone, foot-free, to follow a wandering wisp-light.
For every day at sundown, at the first beacon's gleam,
She calls the gulls her brothers and keeps a tryst with them.
"O gulls, white gulls, what see you beyond the sloping blue?

And where away's the Snowflake, she's so long overdue?"
Then, as the gloaming settles, the hilltop stars emerge
And watch that plaintive figure patrol the dark sea verge.
She follows the marsh fire; her heart laughs and is glad;
She knows that light to seaward is her own sailor lad!
What are these tales they tell her of wreckage on the shore?
Delay but makes his coming the nearer than before!
Surely her eyes have sighted his schooner in the lift!
But the great tide he homes on sets with an outward drift.
So will-o'-the-wisp deludes her till dawn, and she turns home
In unperturbed assurance, "To-morrow he will come."
This is the tale of Malyn, whom sudden grief so marred.
And still each lovely summer resumes that sweet regard,—
The old unvexed eternal indifference to pain;
The sea sings in the marshes, and June comes back again.
All night the lapsing rivers lisp in the long dike grass,
And many memories whisper the sea-winds as they pass;
The tides disturb the silence; but not a hindrance bars
The wash of time, where founder even the galleon stars.
And all night long wherever the moving waters gleam,
The little hills hearken, hearken, the great hills hear and dream.

THE NANCY'S PRIDE

On the long slow heave of a lazy sea,
To the flap of an idle sail,
The Nancy's Pride went out on the tide;
And the skipper stood by the rail.

All down, all down by the sleepy town,
With the hollyhocks a-row
In the little poppy gardens,
The sea had her in tow.

They let her slip by the breathing rip,
Where the bell is never still,
And over the sounding harbor bar,
And under the harbor hill.

She melted into the dreaming noon,
Out of the drowsy land,
In sight of a flag of goldy hair,
To the kiss of a girlish hand.

For the lass who hailed the lad who sailed,
Was—who but his April bride?

And of all the fleet of Grand Latite,
Her pride was the Nancy's Pride.

So the little vessel faded down
With her creaking boom a-swing,
Till a wind from the deep came up with a creep,
And caught her wing and wing.

She made for the lost horizon line,
Where the clouds a-castled lay,
While the boil and seethe of the open sea
Hung on her frothing way.

She lifted her hull like a breasting gull
Where the rolling valleys be,
And dipped where the shining porpoises
Put ploughshares through the sea.

A fading sail on the far sea-line,
About the turn of the tide,
As she made for the Banks on her maiden cruise,
Was the last of the Nancy's Pride.

To-day a boy with goldy hair,
In a garden of Grand Latite,
From his mother's knee looks out to sea
For the coming of the fleet.

They all may home on a sleepy tide,
To the flap of the idle sail;
But it's never again the Nancy's Pride
That answers a human hail.

They all may home on a sleepy tide
To the sag of an idle sheet;
But it's never again the Nancy's Pride
That draws men down the street.

On the Banks to-night a fearsome sight
The fishermen behold,
Keeping the ghost watch in the moon
When the small hours are cold.

When the light wind veers, and the white fog clears,
They see by the after rail
An unknown schooner creeping up
With mildewed spar and sail.

Her crew lean forth by the rotting shrouds,
With the Judgment in their face;
And to their mates' "God save you!"
Have never a word of grace.

Then into the gray they sheer away,
On the awful polar tide;
And the sailors know they have seen the wraith
Of the missing Nancy's Pride.

ARNOLD, MASTER OF THE SCUD

There's a schooner out from Kingsport,
Through the morning's dazzle-gleam,
Snoring down the Bay of Fundy
With a norther on her beam.

How the tough wind springs to wrestle,
When the tide is on the flood!
And between them stands young daring—
Arnold, master of the Scud.

He is only "Martin's youngster,"
To the Minas coasting fleet,
"Twelve year old, and full of Satan
As a nut is full of meat."

With a wake of froth behind him,
And the gold green waste before,
Just as though the sea this morning
Were his boat pond by the door,

Legs a-straddle, grips the tiller
This young waif of the old sea;
When the wind comes harder, only
Laughs "Hurrah!" and holds her free.

Little wonder, as you watch him
With the dash in his blue eye,
Long ago his father called him
"Arnold, Master," on the sly,

While his mother's heart foreboded
Reckless father makes rash son.
So to-day the schooner carries
Just these two whose will is one.

Now the wind grows moody, shifting
Point by point into the east.
Wing and wing the Scud is flying
With her scuppers full of yeast.

And the father's older wisdom
On the sea-line has descried,
Like a stealthy cloud-bank making
Up to windward with the tide,

Those tall navies of disaster,
The pale squadrons of the fog,
That maraud this gray world border
Without pilot, chart, or log,

Ranging wanton as marooners
From Minudie to Manan.
"Heave to, and we'll reef, my master!"
Cries he; when no will of man

Spills the foresail, but a clumsy
Wind-flaw with a hand like stone
Hurls the boom round. In an instant
Arnold, Master, there alone

Sees a crushed corpse shot to seaward,
With the gray doom in its face;
And the climbing foam receives it
To its everlasting place.

What does Arnold, Master, think you?
Whimper like a child for dread?
That's not Arnold. Foulest weather
Strongest sailors ever bred.

And this slip of taut sea-faring
Grows a man who throttles fear.
Let the storm and dark in spite now
Do their worst with valor here!

Not a reef and not a shiver,
While the wind jeers in her shrouds,
And the flauts of foam and sea-fog
Swarm upon her deck in crowds,

Flies the Scud like a mad racer;
And with iron in his frown,

Holding hard by wrath and dreadnought,
Arnold, Master, rides her down.

Let the taffrail shriek through foam-heads!
Let the licking seas go glut
Elsewhere their old hunger, baffled!
Arnold's making for the Gut.

Cleft sheer down, the sea-wall mountains
Give that one port on the coast;
Made, the Basin lies in sunshine!
Missed, the little Scud is lost!

Come now, fog-horn, let your warning
Rip the wind to starboard there!
Suddenly that burly-throated
Welcome ploughs the cumbered air.

The young master hauls a little,
Crowds her up and sheets her home,
Heading for the narrow entry
Whence the safety signals come.

Then the wind lulls, and an eddy
Tells of ledges, where away;
Veers the Scud, sheet free, sun breaking,
Through the rifts, and—there's the bay!

Like a bird in from the storm-beat,
As the summer sun goes down,
Slows the schooner to her moorings
By the wharf at Digby town.

All the world next morning wondered.
Largest letters, there it stood,
"Storm in Fundy. A Boy's Daring.
Arnold, Master of the Scud."

THE SHIPS OF ST. JOHN

Smile, you inland hills and rivers!
Flush, you mountains in the dawn!
But my roving heart is seaward
With the ships of gray St. John.

Fair the land lies, full of August,

Meadow island, shingly bar,
Open barns and breezy twilight,
Peace and the mild evening star.

Gently now this gentlest country
The old habitude takes on,
But my wintry heart is outbound
With the great ships of St. John.

Once in your wide arms you held me,
Till the man-child was a man,
Canada, great nurse and mother
Of the young sea-roving clan.

Always your bright face above me
Through the dreams of boyhood shone;
Now far alien countries call me
With the ships of gray St. John.

Swing, you tides, up out of Fundy!
Blow, you white fogs, in from sea!
I was born to be your fellow;
You were bred to pilot me.

At the touch of your strong fingers,
Doubt, the derelict, is gone;
Sane and glad I clear the headland
With the white ships of St. John.

Loyalists, my fathers, builded
This gray port of the gray sea,
When the duty to ideals
Could not let well-being be.

When the breadth of scarlet bunting
Puts the wreath of maple on,
I must cheer too,—slip my moorings
With the ships of gray St. John.

Peerless-hearted port of heroes,
Be a word to lift the world,
Till the many see the signal
Of the few once more unfurled.

Past the lighthouse, past the nunbuoy,
Past the crimson rising sun,
There are dreams go down the harbor
With the tall ships of St. John.

In the morning I am with them
As they clear the island bar,—
Fade, till speck by speck the midday
Has forgotten where they are.

But I sight a vaster sea-line,
Wider lee-way, longer run,
Whose discoverers return not
With the ships of gray St. John.

THE KING OF YS

Wild across the Breton country,
Fabled centuries ago,
Riding from the black sea border,
Came the squadrons of the snow.

Piping dread at every latch-hole,
Moaning death at every sill,
The white Yule came down in vengeance
Upon Ys, and had its will.

Walled and dreamy stood the city,
Wide and dazzling shone the sea,
When the gods set hand to smother
Ys, the pride of Brittany.

Morning drenched her towers in purple;
Light of heart were king and fool;
Fair forebode the merrymaking
Of the seven days of Yule.

Laughed the king, "Once more, my mistress,
Time and place and joy are one!"
Bade the balconies with banners
Match the splendor of the sun;

Eyes of urchins shine with silver,
And with gold the pavement ring;
Bade the war-horns sound their bravest
In The Mistress of the King.

Mountebanks and ballad-mongers
And all strolling traffickers
Should block up the market corners

With none other name than hers.

Laughed the fool, "To-day, my Folly,
Thou shalt be the king of Ys!"
O wise fool! How long must wisdom
Under motley hold her peace?

Then the storm came down. The valleys
Wailed and ciphered to the dune
Like huge organ pipes; a midnight
Stalked those gala streets at noon;

And the sea rose, rocked and tilted
Like a beaker in the hand,
Till the moon-hung tide broke tether
And stampeded in for land.

All day long with doom portentous,
Shreds of pennons shrieked and flew
Over Ys; and black fear shuddered
On the hearthstone all night through.

Fear, which freezes up the marrow
Of the heart, from door to door
Like a plague went through the city,
And filled up the devil's score;

Filled her tally of the craven,
To the sea-wind's dismal note;
While a panic superstition
Took the people by the throat.

As with morning still the sea rose
With vast wreckage on the tide,
And their pasture rills, grown rivers,
Thundered in the mountain side,

"Vengeance, vengeance, gods to vengeance!"
Rose a storm of muttering;
And the human flood came pouring
To the palace of the king.

"Save, O king, before we perish
In the whirlpools of the sea,
Ys thy city, us thy people!"
Growled the king then, "What would ye?"

But his wolf's eyes talked defiance,

And his bearded mouth meant scorn.
"O our king, the gods are angry;
And no longer to be borne

"Is the shameless face that greets us
From thy windows, at thy side,
Smiling infamy. And therefore
Thou shall take her up, and ride

"Down with her into the sea's mouth,
And there leave her; else we die,
And thy name goes down to story
A new word for cruelty."

Ah, but she was fair, this woman!
Warm and flaxen waved her hair;
Her blue Breton eyes made summer
In that bleak December air.

There she stood whose burning beauty
Made the world's high roof tree ring,
A white poppy tall and wind-blown
In the garden of the king.

Her throat shook, but not with terror;
Her eyes swam, but not with fear;
While her two hands caught and clung to
The one man they had found dear.

"Lord and lover,"—thus she smiled him
Her last word,—"it shall be so,
Only the sea's arms shall hold me,
When from out thine arms I go."

Swore he, "By the gods, my mistress,
Thou shall have queen's burial.
Pearls and amber shall thy tomb be;
Shot with gold and green thy pall.

"And a million-throated chorus
Shall take up thy dirge to-night;
Where thy slumber's starry watch-fires
Shall a thousand years be bright."

Then they brought the coal-black stallion,
Chafing on the bit. Astride
Sprang the young king; shouted, "Way there!"
Caught the girl up to his side;

And a path through that scared rabble
Rode in pageant to the sea.
And the coal-black mane was mingled
With gold hair against his knee.

Sure as the wild gulls make seaward,
From the west gate to the beach
Rode these two for whom now freedom
Landward lay beyond their reach.

And the great horse, scenting peril,
Snorted at the flying spume,
Flicked with courage, as how often,
When the tides were racing doom,

Ridden, he had plunged to rescue
From that seething icy hell
Some poor sailor wrecked a-fishing
On the coast. What fears should quell

That high spirit? Knee to shoulder,
King and stallion reared and sprang
Clear above the long white combers
And that turmoil's iron clang.

What a launching! For a moment,
While the tempest held its breath
And a thousand eyes looked wonder,
Swimming in that trough of death,

Steering seaward through the welter,
Ere they settled out of sight,
Waved above them one gold streamer.
Valor, bid the world good-night!...

Not a trace, while the long summers
Warm the heart of Brittany,
Save one stone of Ys, as remnant,
For a white mark in the sea.

THE KELPIE RIDERS

I

Buried alive in calm Rochelle,

Six in a row by a crystal well,

All Summer long on Bareau Fen
Slumber and sleep the Kelpie men;

By the side of each to cheer his ghost,
A flagon of foam with a crumpet of frost.

Hear me, friends, for the years are fleet;
Soon I leave the noise and the street

For the silent uncompanioned way
Where the inn is cold and the night is gray.

But noon is warm and the world is still
Where the Kelpie riders have their will.

For never a wind dare stir or stray
Over those marshes salt and gray;

No bit of shade as big as your hand
To traverse or trammel the sleeping land,

Save where a dozen poplars fleck
The long gray grass and the well's blue beck.

Yet you mark their leaves are blanched and sear,
Whispering daft at a nameless fear.

While round the hole of one is a rune,
Black in the wash of the bleaching noon.

"Ride, for the wind is awake and away.
Sleep, for the harvest grain is gray."

No word more. And many a mile,
A ghostly bivouac rank and file,

They sleep to-day on the marshes wide;
Some far night they will wake and ride.

Once they were riders hot with speed,
"Kelpie, Kelpie, gallop at need!"

With hills of the barren sea to roam,
Housing their horses on the foam.

But earth is cool and the hush is long

Beneath the lull of the slumber song

The crickets falter and strive to tell
To the dragon-fly of the crystal well;

And love is a forgotten jest,
Where the Kelpie riders take their rest,

And blossoming grasses hour by hour
Burn in the bud and freeze in the flower.

But never again shall their roving be
On the shifting hills of the tumbling sea,

With the salt, and the rain, and the glad desire
Strong as the wind and pure as fire.

II

One doomful night in the April tide
With riot of brooks on the mountain side,

The goblin maidens of the hills
Went forth to the revel-call of the rills.

Many as leaves of the falling year,
To the swing of a ballad wild and clear

They held the plain and the uplands high;
And the merry-dancers held the sky.

The Kelpie riders abroad on the sea
Caught sound of that call of eerie glee,

Over their prairie waste and wan;
And the goblin maidens tolled them on.

The yellow eyes and the raven hair
And the tawny arms blown fresh and bare,

Were more than a mortal might behold
And live with the saints for a crown of gold.

The Kelpie riders were stricken sore;
They wavered, and wheeled, and rode for the shore.

"Kelpie, Kelpie, treble your stride!

Never again on the sea we ride.

"Kelpie, Kelpie, out of the storm;
On, for the fields of earth are warm!"

Knee to knee they are riding in:
"Brother, brother,—the goblin kin!"

The meadows rocked as they clomb the scaur;
The pines re-echo for evermore

The sound of the host of Kelpie men;
But the windflowers died on Bareau Fen.

Over the marshes all night long
The stars went round to a riding song:

"Kelpie, Kelpie, carry us through!"
And the goblin maidens danced thereto.

Till dawn,—and the revel died with a shout,
For the ocean riders were wearied out.

They looked, and the grass was warm and soft;
The dreamy clouds went over aloft;

A gloom of pines on the weather verge
Had the lulling sound of their own white surge;

A whip-poor-will, far from their din,
Was saying his litanies therein.

Then voices neither loud nor deep:
"Tired, so tired; sleep! ah, sleep!

"The stars are calm, and the earth is warm,
But the sea for an earldom is given to storm.

"Come now, inherit the houses of doom;
Your fields of the sun shall be harried of gloom."

They laid them down; but over long
They rest,—for the goblin maids are strong.

The sun goes round; and Bareau Fen
Is a door of earth on the Kelpie men,—

Buried at dawn, asleep, unslain,

With not a mound on the sunny plain,

Hard by the walls of calm Rochelle,
Row on row by the crystal well.

And never again they are free to ride
Through all the years on the tossing tide,

Barred from the breast of the barren foam,
Where the heart within them is yearning home,—

For one long drench of the surf to quell
The cursing doom of the goblin spell.

Only, when bugling snows alight
To smother the marshes stark and white,

Or a low red moon peers over the rim
Of a winter twilight crisp and dim,

With a sound of drift on the buried lands,
The goblin maidens loose their hands;

A wind comes down from the sheer blue North;
And the Kelpie riders get them forth.

III

Twice have I been on Bareau Fen,
But the son of my son is a man since then.

Once as a lad I used to bear
St. Louis' cross through the chapel square,

Leading the choristers' surpliced file
Slow up the dusk Cathedral aisle.

I was the boy of all Rochelle
The pure old father trusted well.

But one clear night in the winter's heart,
I wandered out to that place apart.

The shafts of smoke went up to the stars,
Straight as the Northern Streamer spars,

From the town's white roofs, so still it was.

The night in her dream let no word pass,

Nor ever a breath that one could feel;
Only the snow shrieked under my heel.

Yet it seemed when I reached the poplar hole,
The ghost of a voice was crying, "Skoal!

"Rouse thee and drink, for the well is sweet,
And the crystal snow is good to eat!"

I heeded little, but stooped on my knee,
And ate of a handful dreamily.

'Twas cool to the mouth and slaking at first,
But the lure of it was ill for thirst.

The voice cried, "Soul of the mortal span,
Art thou not of the Kelpie clan?"

"What are you doing there in the ground,
Kelpie rider, and never a sound

"To roam the night but the ghost of a cry?"
Ringing and swift there came reply,

"He is asleep where thou art afraid,
In the tawny arms of a goblin maid!"

Then I knew the voice was the voice of a girl,
And I marvelled much (while a little swirl

Of snow leaped up far off on the plain
Of sparkling dust and died again),

For what do the cloisters know, think ye,
Of women's ways? They be hard to see.

Again the voice cried, "Kin of my kin,
The child of the Sun shall win, shall win!"

'Twas an evil weird that so befell;
Yet I leaned and drank of the bubbling well.

I looked for my face in the crystal spring,
But the face that flickered there was a thing

To make the nape of your neck grow chill,

And every vein surge back and thrill

With a passion for something not their own—
In a life their life has never known.

For raven hair and eyes like the sun
Are merry but dour to look upon.

She smiled through her lashes under the wave,
And my soul went forth her bartered slave.

I swore, "By St. Louis, I'll come to thee,
Though I ride to my doom in the gulfs of the sea!

"Thy Kelpie rider shall wake and rue
His ruined life in the loss of you."

Then I fled in the start of a terror of joy,
O'er leagues where a legion might deploy;

For the acres of snow were level and hard,
Every flake like a crystal shard.

I was the runner of all Rochelle,
Could run with the hounds on Haric Fell;

And something stark as a gust of the sea
Had a grip of the whimsy boy in me.

I ran like the drift on the ice low curled
When the winds of Yule are abroad on the world.

Sudden, the beat of a throbbing sound
Lost in the core of the blue profound:

"Kelpie, Kelpie, Kelpie, come!"
Was it my heart?—But my heart was numb.

"Kelpie, Kelpie!" Was it the sea?
Far on, at the verge of Bareau lea,

I saw like an army, shield and casque,
The breakers roll in the Roads of Basque.

"Kelpie, Kelpie!" Was it the wolves?
In the dusk of pines where night dissolves

To streamers and stars through the mountain gorge,

I heard the blast of a giant forge.

Then I knew the wind was awake from the North,
And the ocean riders were freed and forth.

Time, there is time (now gallop, my heart!)
Ere the black riders disperse and depart.

The dawn is late, but the dawn comes round,
And Fleetfoot Jean has the wind of a hound.

The hue and cry of the Kelpie horde
Was growing and grim on that white seaboard.

It rolled and gathered and died and grew
Far off to the rear; a smile thereto

I turned; a fathom behind my ear
A rider rode with a shadowy leer.

I sickened and sped. He laughed aloud,
"Wind for a mourner, snow for a shroud!"

On and on, half blown, half blind,
Shadow and self, and the wind behind!

I slackened, he slackened; I fled, he flew;
In a swirl of snow-drift all night through

I scoured along the gusty fen,
A quarry for hunting Kelpie men.

But only one could hold at my side:
"Brother, brother, I love thy stride.

"Wilt thou follow thy whim to win
My merry maid of the goblin kin?"

I swerved from my trail, for he haunted my ear
With his moaning jibe and his shadowy leer.

So by good hap as we sped it fell,
I fetched a circuit back for the well.

Like a spilth of spume on the crest of the bore
When the combing tides make in for shore,

That runner ran whose love was a wraith;

But the rider rode with revenge in his teeth.

Another league, and I touch the goal,—
The mystic rune on the poplar bole,—

When the dusky eyes and the raven hair
And the lithe brown arms shall greet me there.

I ran like a harrier on the trace
In the leash of that ghoul, and the wind gave chase.

A furlong now; I caught the gleam
Of the bubbling well with its tiny stream;

An arrowy burst; I cleared the beck;
And—the Kelpie rider bestrode my neck.

Dawn, the still red winter dawn;
I awoke on the plain; the wind was gone;—

All gracious and good as when God made
The living creatures, and none was afraid.

I stooped to drink of the wholesome spring
Under the poplars whispering:

Face to my face in that water clear—
The Kelpie rider's jabbering leer!

Ah, God! not me: I was never so!
Sainted Louis, who can know

The lords of life from the slaves of death?
What help avail the speeding breath

Of the spirit that knows not self's abode,—
When the soul is lost that knows not God?

I turned me home by St. Louis' Hall,
Where the red sun burns on the windows tall.

And I thought the world was strange and wild,
And God with his altar only a child.

IV

Again one year in the prime of June,

I came to the well in the heated noon,

Leaving Rochelle with its red roof tiles
By the Pottery Gate before St. Giles,—

There where the flower market is,
Where every morning up from Duprisse

The flower girls come by the long white lane
That skirts the edge of Bareau plain;—

To the North, the city wall in the sun,
To the left, the fen where the eye may run

And have its will of the blazing blue.
The while I loitered the market through,

Halting a moment to converse
With old Babette who had been my nurse,

There passed through the stalls a woman, bright
With a kirtle of cinnabar and white

Among the kerseys blue; and I said,
"Who is it, Babette, with lifted head,

"And the startled look, possessed and strange,
Under the paint—secure from change?"

"Ah, 'Sieur Jean, do ye not ken
Of the eerie folk of Bareau Fen?"

I blenched, and she knew too well I wist
The fearsome fate of the goblin tryst.

"The street is a cruel home, 'Sieur Jean,
But a weird uncanny drives her on.

"'Tis a bitter tale for Christian folk,
How once she dreamed, and how she woke."

"Ay, ay!" I passed and reached the spring
Where the poplars kept their whispering,

Hid for an hour in the shade,
In the rank marsh grass of a tiny glade.

There crossed the moor from the town afar,

In kirtle of white and cinnabar,

A wanderer on that plain of tears,
Bowed with a burden not of the years,

As one that goeth sorrowing
For many an unforgotten thing.

To the crystal well as the sun drew low
There came that harridan of woe.

She stooped to drink; I heard her cry:
"Ah, God, how tired out am I!

"I called him by the dearest name
A girl may call; I have my shame.

"'Yet death is crueller than life,'
Once they said, 'for all the strife.'

"And so I lived; but the wild will,
Broken and bitter, drives to ill.

"And now I know, what no one saith,
That love is crueller than death.

"How I did love him! Is love too high,
My God, for such lost folk as I?"

Her tears went down to the grass by the well,
In that passion of grief, and where they fell

Windflowers trembled pale and white.
A craven I crept away from the sight;

And turned me home to St. Louis' Hall,
Where the sunflowers burn by the eastern wall.

The vesper frankincense that day
Rose to the rafters and melted away,

And was no more than a cloud that stirs
Among the spires of Norway firs.

And I said, "The holy solitude
Of the hoary crypt and the wild green wood

"Are one to the God I have never known,

Whose kingdom has neither bourn nor throne."

V

Now I am old, and the years delay;
But I know, I know, there will come a day,—

When April is over the Norland town.
And the loosened brooks from the hills go down,

When tears have quenched the sorrow of time,—
Wherein the earth shall rebuild her prime,

And the houses of dark be overthrown;
When the goblin maids shall love their own,—

Their arms forever unlaced from their hold
Of the earls of the sea on that alien wold,—

And the feckless light of their golden eyes
Shall forget the desire that made them wise;

When the hands of the foam shall beckon and flee.
And the Kelpie riders ride for the sea;

And the whip-poor-will the whole night long
Repeat his litanies of song,

Till morning whiten the world again,
And the flowers revive on Bareau Fen,

Over the acres of calm Rochelle
Fresh by the stream of the crystal well.

NOONS OF POPPY

Noons of poppy, noons of poppy,
Scarlet leagues along the sea;
Flaxen hair afloat in sunlight,
Love, come down the world to me!

There's a Captain I must ship with,
(Heart, that day be far from now!)
Wears his dark command in silence
With the sea-frost on his brow.

Noons of poppy, noons of poppy,
Purple shadows by the sea;
How should love take thought to wonder
What the destined port may be?

Nay, if love have joy for shipmate
For a night-watch or a year,
Dawn will light o'er Lonely Haven,
Heart to happy heart, as here.

Noons of poppy, noons of poppy,
Scarlet acres by the sea
Burning to the blue above them;
Love, the world is full for me.

LEGENDS OF LOST HAVEN

There are legends of Lost Haven,
Come, I know not whence, to me,
When the wind is in the clover,
When the sun is on the sea.

There are rumors in the pine-tops,
There are whispers in the grass;
And the flocking crows at nightfall
Bring home hints of things that pass

Out upon the broad dike yonder,
All day long beneath the sun,
Where the tall ships cloud and settle
Down the sea-curve, one by one.

And the crickets in fine chorus—
Every slim and tiny reed—
Strive to chord the broken rhythmus
Of the world, and half succeed.

There are myriad traditions
Treasured by the talking rain;
And with memories the moonlight
Walks the cold and silent plain.

Where the river tells his hill-tales
To the lone complaining bar,
Where the midgets thread their dances

To the yellow twilight star,

Where the blossom bends to hearken
To the bee with velvet bands,
There are chronicles enciphered
Of the yet uncharted lands.

All the musical marauders
Of the berry and the bloom
Sing the lure of soul's illusion
Out of darkness, out of doom.

But the sure and great evangel
Comes when half alone I hear,
At the rosy door of silence,
Love, the lord of speech, draw near.

Then for once across the threshold,
Darkling spirit, thou art free,—
As thy hope is every ship makes
Some lost haven of the sea.

THE SHADOW BOATSWAIN

Don't you know the sailing orders?
It is time to put to sea,
And the stranger in the harbor
Sends a boat ashore for me.

With the thunder of her canvas
Coming on the wind again,
I can hear the Shadow Boatswain
Piping to his shadow men.

Is it firelight or morning,
That red flicker on the floor?
Your good-by was braver, sweetheart,
When I sailed away before.

Think of this last lovely summer!
Love, what ails the wind to-night?
What's he saying in the chimney
Turns your berry cheek so white?

What a morning! How the sunlight
Sparkles on the outer bay,

Where the brig lies waiting for me
To trip anchor and away!

That's the Doomkeel. You may know her
By her clean run aft; and, then,
Don't you hear the Shadow Boatswain
Piping to his shadow men?

Off the freshening sea to windward,
Is it a white tern I hear
Shrilling in the gusty weather
Where the far sea-line is clear?

What a morning for departure!
How your blue eyes melt and shine!
Will you watch us from the headland
Till we sink below the line?

I can see the wind already
Steer the scurf marks of the tide,
As we slip the wake of being
Down the sloping world and wide.

I can feel the vasty mountains
Heave and settle under me,
And the Doomkeel veer and shudder,
Crumbling on the hollow sea.

There's a call, as when a white gull
Cries and beats across the blue;
That must be the Shadow Boatswain
Piping to his shadow crew.

There's a boding sound, like winter
When the pines begin to quail;
That must be the gray wind moaning
In the belly of the sail.

I can feel the icy fingers
Creeping in upon my bones;
There must be a berg to windward
Somewhere in these border zones.

Stir the fire.... I love the sunlight,—
Always loved my shipmate sun.
How the sunflowers beckon to me
From the dooryard one by one!

How the royal lady roses
Strew this summer world of ours!
There'll be none in Lonely Haven;
It is too far north for flowers.

There, sweetheart! And I must leave you.
What should touch my wife with tears?
There's no danger with the Master;
He has sailed the sea for years.

With the sea-wolves on her quarter,
And a white bone in her teeth,
He will steer the shadow cruiser,
Dark before and doom beneath,

Down the last expanse, till morning
Flares above the broken sea,
And the midnight storm is over,
And the Isles are close alee.

So some twilight, when your roses
Are all blown and it is June,
You will turn your blue eyes seaward
Through the white dusk of the moon,

Wondering, as that far sea-cry
Comes upon the wind again,
And you hear the Shadow Boatswain
Piping to his shadow men.

THE MASTER OF THE ISLES

There is rumor in Dark Harbor,
And the folk are all astir;
For a stranger in the offing
Draws them down to gaze at her,

In the gray of early morning,
Black against the orange streak,
Making in below the ledges,
With no colors at her peak.

Something makes their hearts uneasy
As they watch the long black hull,
For she brings the storm behind her
While before her there is lull.

With no pilot and unspoken,
Where the dancing breakers are,
Presently she veers and races
In across the roaring bar,—

Rounds and luffs and comes to anchor,
While the wharf begins to throng.
Silence falls upon the women.
And misgiving stirs the strong.

Then with some obscure foreboding,
As a gray-haired watcher smiles,
They perceive the fearless captain
Is the Master of the Isles.

They recall the bleak December
Many streaming years ago,
When the stranger had been sighted
Driving shoreward with the snow;

When the Master came among them
With his calm and courtly pride,
And had sailed away at sundown
With pale Dora for his bride;

How again he came one summer
When the herring schools were late,
And had cleared before the morning
With old Alec's son for mate.

There was glamour with the Master;
He had tales of far-off seas;
But his habit and demeanor
Were of other lands than these.

He had never made the Harbor
But there sailed away with him
Wife or child or friend or lover,
Leaving eyes to strain and swim,—

Strain and wait for their returning;
Yet they never had come back;
For the pale wake of the Master
Is a wandering, fading track.

Just beyond our utmost fathom
Is the anchorage we crave,

But the Master knows the soundings
By the reach of every wave.

Just beyond the last horizon,
Vague upon the weather-gleam,
Loom the Faroff Isles forever,
The tradition of a dream.

There a white and brooding summer
Haunts upon the gray sea-plain,
Where the gray sea-winds are quiet
At the sources of the rain.

There where all world-weary dreamers
Get them forth to their release,
Lie the colonies of the kindred,
In the provinces of peace.

Thither in the stormy sunset
Will the Master sail to-night;
And the village will be silent
When he drops below the light.

Not a soul on all the hillside
But will watch her when she clears,
Dreaming of the Port o' Strangers
In the roadstead of the years.

"Port o' Strangers, Port o' Strangers!"
"Where away?" "On the weather bow."
"Drive her down the closing distance!"...
That's to-morrow, but not now.

What imperial adventure
Some wide morning it will be,
Sweeping in to Lonely Haven
From the chartless round of sea!

How imposing a departure,
While this little harbor smiles,
Steering for the outer sea-rim
With the Master of the Isles!

THE LAST WATCH

Comrades, comrades, have me buried

Like a warrior of the sea,
With a flag across my breast
And my sword upon my knee.

Steering out from vanished headlands
For a harbor on no chart,
With the winter in the rigging,
With the ice-wind in my heart,

Down the bournless slopes of sea-room,
With the long gray wake behind,
I have sailed my cruiser steady
With no pilot but the wind.

Battling with relentless pirates
From the lower seas of Doom,
I have kept the colors flying
Through the roar of drift and gloom.

Scudding where the shadow foemen
Hang about us grim and stark,
Broken spars and shredded canvas,
We are racing for the dark.

Sped and blown abaft the sunset
Like a shriek the storm has caught;
But the helm is lashed to windward,
And the sails are sheeted taut.

Comrades, comrades, have me buried
Like a warrior of the night.
I can hear the bell-buoy calling
Down below the harbor light

Steer in shoreward, loose the signal,
The last watch has been cut short;
Speak me kindly to the islesmen,
When we make the foreign port.

We shall make it ere the morning
Rolls the fog from strait and bluff;
Where the offing crimsons eastward
There is anchorage enough.

How I wander in my dreaming!
Are we northing nearer home,
Or outbound for fresh adventure
On the reeling plains of foam?

North I think it is, my comrades,
Where one heart-beat counts for ten,
Where the loving hand is loyal,
And the women's sons are men;

Where the red auroras tremble
When the polar night is still,
Lighting home the worn seafarers
To their haven in the hill.

Comrades, comrades, have me buried
Like a warrior of the North.
Lower me the long-boat, stay me
In your arms, and bear me forth;

Lay me in the sheets and row me,
With the tiller in my hand,
Row me in below the beacon
Where my sea-dogs used to land.

Has your captain lost his cunning
After leading you so far?
Row me your last league, my sea-kings;
It is safe within the bar.

Shoulder me and house me hillward,
Where the field-lark makes his bed,
So the gulls can wheel above me,
All day long when I am dead;

Where the keening wind can find me
With the April rain for guide,
And come crooning her old stories
Of the kingdoms of the tide.

Comrades, comrades, have me buried
Like a warrior of the sun;
I have carried my sealed orders
Till the last command is done.

Kiss me on the cheek for courage,
(There is none to greet me home,)
Then farewell to your old lover
Of the thunder of the foam;

For the grass is full of slumber
In the twilight world for me,

And my tired hands are slackened
From their toiling on the sea.

OUTBOUND

A lonely sail in the vast sea-room,
I have put out for the port of gloom.

The voyage is far on the trackless tide,
The watch is long, and the seas are wide.

The headlands blue in the sinking day
Kiss me a hand on the outward way.

The fading gulls, as they dip and veer,
Lift me a voice that is good to hear.

The great winds come, and the heaving sea,
The restless mother, is calling me.

The cry of her heart is lone and wild,
Searching the night for her wandered child.

Beautiful, weariless mother of mine,
In the drift of doom I am here, I am thine.

Beyond the fathom of hope or fear,
From bourn to bourn of the dusk I steer,

Swept on in the wake of the stars, in the stream
Of a roving tide, from dream to dream.

Bliss Carman - An Appreciation

How many Canadians—how many even among the few who seek to keep themselves informed of the best in contemporary literature, who are ever on the alert for the new voices—realise, or even suspect, that this Northern land of theirs has produced a poet of whom it may be affirmed with confidence and assurance that he is of the great succession of English poets? Yet such—strange and unbelievable though it may seem—is in very truth the case, that poet being (to give him his full name) William Bliss Carman. Canada has full right to be proud of her poets, a small body though they are; but not only does Mr. Carman stand high and clear above them all—his place (and time cannot but confirm and justify the assertion) is among those men whose poetry is the shining glory of that great English literature which is our common heritage.

If any should ask why, if what has been just said is so, there has been—as must be admitted—no general recognition of the fact in the poet's home land, I would answer that there are various and plausible, if not good, reasons for it.

First of all, the poet, as thousands more of our young men of ambition and confidence have done, went early to the United States, and until recently, except for rare and brief visits to his old home down by the sea, has never returned to Canada—though for all that, I am able to state, on his own authority, he is still a Canadian citizen. Then all his books have had their original publication in the United States, and while a few of them have subsequently carried the imprints of Canadian publishers, none of these can be said ever to have made any special effort to push their sale. Another reason for the fact above mentioned is that Mr. Carman has always scorned to advertise himself, while his work has never been the subject of the log-rolling and booming which the work of many another poet has had—to his ultimate loss. A further reason is that he follows a rule of his own in preparing his books for publication. Most poets publish a volume of their work as soon as, through their industry and perseverance, they have material enough on hand to make publication desirable in their eyes. Not so with Mr. Carman, however, his rule being not to publish until he has done sufficient work of a certain general character or key to make a volume. As a result, you cannot fully know or estimate his work by one book, or two books, or even half a dozen; you must possess or be familiar with every one of the score and more volumes which contain his output of poetry before you can realise how great and how many-sided is his genius.

It is a common remark on the part of those who respond readily to the vigorous work of Kipling, or Masefield, even our own Service, that Bliss Carman's poetry has no relation to or concern with ordinary, everyday life. One would suppose that most persons who cared for poetry at all turned to it as a relief from or counter to the burdens and vexations of the daily round; but in any event, the remark referred to seems to me to indicate either the most casual acquaintance with Mr. Carman's work, or a complete misunderstanding and misapprehension of the meaning of it. I grant that you will find little or nothing in it all to remind you of the grim realities and vexing social problems of this modern existence of ours; but to say or to suggest that these things do not exist for Mr. Carman is to say or to suggest something which is the reverse of true. The truth is, he is aware of them as only one with the sensitive organism of a poet can be; but he does not feel that he has a call or mission to remedy them, and still less to sing of them. He therefore leaves the immediate problems of the day to those who choose, or are led, to occupy themselves therewith, and turns resolutely away to dwell upon those things which for him possess infinitely greater importance.

"What are they?" one who knows Mr. Carman only as, say, a lyrist of spring or as a singer of the delights of vagabondia probably will ask in some wonder. Well, the things which concern him above all, I would answer, are first, and naturally, the beauty and wonder of this world of ours, and next the mystery of the earthly pilgrimage of the human soul out of eternity and back into it again.

The poems in the present volume—which, by the way, can boast the high honor of being the very first regular Canadian edition of his work—will be evidence ample and conclusive to every reader, I am sure, of the place which

The perennial enchanted
Lovely world and all its lore

occupy in the heart and soul of Bliss Carman, as well as of the magical power with which he is able to convey the deep and unfailing satisfaction and delight which they possess for him. They, however, represent his latest period (he has had three well-defined periods), comprising selections from three of his last published volumes: The Rough Rider, Echoes from Vagabondia, and April Airs, together with a number of new poems, and do not show, except here and there and by hints and flashes, how great is his preoccupation with the problem of man's existence—

—the hidden import
Of man's eternal plight.

This is manifest most in certain of his earlier books, for in these he turns and returns to the greatest of all the problems of man almost constantly, probing, with consummate and almost unrivalled use of the art of expression, for the secret which surely, he clearly feels, lies hidden somewhere, to be discovered if one could but pierce deeply enough. Pick up Behind the Arras, and as you turn over page after page you cannot but observe how incessantly the poet's mind—like the minds of his two great masters, Browning and Whitman—works at this problem. In "Behind the Arras," the title poem; "In the Wings," "The Crimson House," "The Lodger," "Beyond the Gamut," "The Juggler"—yes, in every poem in the book—he takes up and handles the strange thing we know as, or call, life, turning it now this way, now that, in an effort to find out its meaning and purpose. He comes but little nearer success in this than do most of the rest of men, of course; but the magical and ever-fresh beauty of his expression, the haunting melody of his lines, the variety of his images and figures and the depth and range of his thought, put his searchings and ponderings in a class by themselves.

Lengthy quotation from Mr. Carman's books is not permitted here, and I must guide myself accordingly, though with reluctance, because I believe that in a study such as this the subject should be allowed to speak for himself as much as possible. In "Behind the Arras" the poet describes the passage from life to death as

A cadence dying down unto its source
In music's course,

and goes on to speak of death as

—the broken rhythm of thought and man,
The sweep and span
Of memory and hope
About the orbit where they still must grope
For wider scope,

To be through thousand springs restored, renewed,
With love imbrued,
With increments of will
Made strong, perceiving unattainment still
From each new skill.

Now follow some verses from "Behind the Gamut," to my mind the poet's greatest single achievement;

As fine sand spread on a disc of silver,

At some chord which bids the motes combine,
Heeding the hidden and reverberant impulse,
Shifts and dances into curve and line,

The round earth, too, haply, like a dust-mote,
Was set whirling her assigned sure way,
Round this little orb of her ecliptic
To some harmony she must obey.

And what of man?

Linked to all his half-accomplished fellows,
Through unfrontiered provinces to range—
Man is but the morning dream of nature,
Roused to some wild cadence weird and strange.

Here, now, are some verses from "Pulvis et Umbra," which is to be found in Mr. Carman's first book, Low Tide on Grand Pré, and in which the poet addresses a moth which a storm has blown into his window:

For man walks the world with mourning
Down to death and leaves no trace,
With the dust upon his forehead,
And the shadow on his face.

Pillared dust and fleeing shadow
As the roadside wind goes by,
And the fourscore years that vanish
In the twinkling of an eye.

"Pillared dust and fleeing shadow." Where in all our English literature will one find the life history of man summed up more briefly and, at the same time, more beautifully, than in that wonderful line? Now follows a companion verse to those just quoted, taken from "Lord of My Heart's Elation," which stands in the forefront of From the Green Book of the Bards. It may be remarked here that while the poet recurs again and again to some favorite thought or idea, it is never in the same words. His expression is always new and fresh, showing how deep and true is his inspiration. Again it is man who is pictured:

A fleet and shadowy column
Of dust and mountain rain,
To walk the earth a moment
And be dissolved again.

But while Mr. Carman's speculations upon life's meaning and the mystery of the future cannot but appeal to the thoughtful-minded, it is as an interpreter of nature that he makes his widest appeal. Bliss Carman, I must say here, and emphatically, is no mere landscape-painter; he never, or scarcely ever, paints a picture of nature for its own sake. He goes beyond the outward aspect of things and interprets or translates for us with less keen senses as only a poet whose feeling for nature is of the deepest and profoundest, who has gone to her whole-heartedly and been taken close to her warm bosom, can do. Is this not evident from these verses from "The Great Return"—originally called "The Pagan's Prayer," and for some inscrutable reason to be found only in the limited Collected Poems, issued in two stately volumes in 1905.

When I have lifted up my heart to thee,
Thou hast ever hearkened and drawn near,
And bowed thy shining face close over me,
Till I could hear thee as the hill-flowers hear.

When I have cried to thee in lonely need,
Being but a child of thine bereft and wrung,
Then all the rivers in the hills gave heed;
And the great hill-winds in thy holy tongue—

That ancient incommunicable speech—
The April stars and autumn sunsets know—
Soothed me and calmed with solace beyond reach
Of human ken, mysterious and low.

Who can read or listen to those moving lines without feeling that Mr. Carman is in very truth a poet of nature—nay, Nature's own poet? But how could he be other when, in "The Breath of the Reed" (From the Green Book of the Bards), he makes the appeal?

Make me thy priest, O Mother,
And prophet of thy mood,
With all the forest wonder
Enraptured and imbued.

As becomes such a poet, and particularly a poet whose birth-month is April, Mr. Carman sings much of the early spring. Again and again he takes up his woodland pipe, and lo! Pan himself and all his train troop joyously before us. Yet the singer's notes for all his singing never become wearied or strident; his airs are ever new and fresh; his latest songs are no less spontaneous and winning than were his first, written how many years ago, while at the same time they have gained in beauty and melody. What heart will not stir to the vibrant music of his immortal "Spring Song," which was originally published in the first Songs from Vagabondia, and the opening verses of which follow?

Make me over, mother April,
When the sap begins to stir!
When thy flowery hand delivers
All the mountain-prisoned rivers,
And thy great heart beats and quivers
To revive the days that were,
Make me over, mother April,
When the sap begins to stir!

Take my dust and all my dreaming,
Count my heart-beats one by one,
Send them where the winters perish;
Then some golden noon recherish

And restore them in the sun,
Flower and scent and dust and dreaming,
With their heart-beats every one!

That poem is sufficient in itself to prove that Bliss Carman has full right and title to be called Spring's own lyrist, though it may be remarked here that not all his spring poems are so unfeignedly joyous. Many of them indeed, have a touch, or more than a touch, of wistfulness, for the poet knows well that sorrow lurks under all joy, deep and well hidden though it may be.

Mr. Carman sings equally finely, though perhaps not so frequently, of summer and the other seasons; but as he has other claims upon our attention, I shall forbear to labor the fact, particularly as the following collection demonstrates it sufficiently. One of those other claims is as a writer of sea poetry. Few poets, it may be said, have pictured the majesty and the mystery, the beauty and the terror of the sea, better than he. His Ballads of Lost Haven is a veritable treasure-house for those whose spirits find kinship in wide expanses of moving waters. One of the best known poems in this volume is "The Gravedigger," which opens thus:

Oh, the shambling sea is a sexton old,
And well his work is done.
With an equal grave for lord and knave,
He buries them every one.

Then hoy and rip, with a rolling hip,
He makes for the nearest shore;
And God, who sent him a thousand ship,
Will send him a thousand more;
But some he'll save for a bleaching grave,
And shoulder them in to shore—
Shoulder them in, shoulder them in,
Shoulder them in to shore.

In "The City of the Sea" (Last Songs from Vagabondia) Mr. Carman speaks of the seabells sounding

The eternal cadence of sea sorrow
For Man's lot and immemorial wrong—
The lost strains that haunt the human dwelling
With the ghost of song.

Elsewhere he speaks of

The great sea, mystic and musical.

And here from another poem is a striking picture:

... the old sea
Seems to whimper and deplore
Mourning like a childless crone
With her sorrow left alone—

The eternal human cry
To the heedless passer-by.

I have said above that Mr. Carman has had three distinct periods, and intimated that the poems in the following collection are of his third period. The first period may be said to be represented by the Low Tide and Behind the Arras volumes, while the second is displayed in the three volumes of Songs from Vagabondia, which he published in association with his friend Richard Hovey. Bliss Carman was from the first too original and individual a poet to be directly influenced by anyone else; but there can be no doubt that his friendship with Hovey helped to turn him from over-preoccupation with mysteries which, for all their greatness, are not for man to solve, to an intenser realisation of the beauty and loveliness of the world about him and of the joys of human fellowship. The result is seen in such poems as "Spring Song," quoted in part above, and his perhaps equally well-known "The Joys of the Road," which appeared in the same volume with that poem, and a few verses from which follow:

Now the joys of the road are chiefly these:
A crimson touch on the hardwood trees;

A vagrant's morning wide and blue,
In early fall, when the wind walks, too;

A shadowy highway cool and brown,
Alluring up and enticing down

From rippled waters and dappled swamp,
From purple glory to scarlet pomp;

The outward eye, the quiet will,
And the striding heart from hill to hill.

Some of the finest of arman's work is contained in his elegiac or memorial poems, in which he commemorates Keats, Shelley, William Blake, Lincoln, Stevenson, and other men for whom he has a kindred feeling, and also friends whom he has loved and lost. Listen to these moving lines from "Non Omnis Moriar," written in memory of Gleeson White, and to be found in Last Songs from Vagabondia:

There is a part of me that knows,
Beneath incertitude and fear,
I shall not perish when I pass
Beyond mortality's frontier;

But greatly having joyed and grieved,
Greatly content, shall hear the sigh
Of the strange wind across the lone
Bright lands of taciturnity.

In patience therefore I await
My friend's unchanged benign regard,—
Some April when I too shall be
Spilt water from a broken shard.

In "The White Gull," written for the centenary of the birth of Shelley in 1892, and included in By the Aurelian Wall, he thus apostrophizes that clear and shining spirit:

O captain of the rebel host,
Lead forth and far!
Thy toiling troopers of the night
Press on the unavailing fight;
The sombre field is not yet lost,
With thee for star.

Thy lips have set the hail and haste
Of clarions free
To bugle down the wintry verge
Of time forever, where the surge
Thunders and trembles on a waste
And open sea.

In "A Seamark," a threnody for Robert Louis Stevenson, which appears in the same volume, the poet hails "R.L.S." (of whose tribe he may be said to be truly one) as

The master of the roving kind,

and goes on:

O all you hearts about the world
In whom the truant gypsy blood,
Under the frost of this pale time,
Sleeps like the daring sap and flood
That dreams of April and reprieve!
You whom the haunted vision drives,
Incredulous of home and ease.
Perfection's lovers all your lives!

You whom the wander-spirit loves
To lead by some forgotten clue
Forever vanishing beyond
Horizon brinks forever new;
Our restless loved adventurer,
On secret orders come to him,
Has slipped his cable, cleared the reef,
And melted on the white sea-rim.

"Perfection's lovers all your lives." Of these, it may be said without qualification, is Bliss Carman himself.

No summary of Mr. Carman's work, however cursory, would be worthy of the name if it omitted mention of his ventures in the realm of Greek myth. From the Book of Myths is made up of work of that sort, every poem in it being full of the beauty of phrase and melody of which Mr. Carman alone has the secret. The finest poems in the book, barring the opening one, "Overlord," are "Daphne," "The Dead Faun," "Hylas," and "At Phædra's Tomb," but I can do no more here than name them, for extracts would fail to reveal their full beauty. And beauty, after all is said, is the first and last thing with Mr. Carman. As he says himself somewhere:

The joy of the hand that hews for beauty
Is the dearest solace under the sun.

And again

The eternal slaves of beauty
Are the masters of the world.

A slave—a happy, willing slave—to beauty is the poet himself, and the world can never repay him for the message of beauty which he has brought it.

Kindred to From the Book of Myths, but much more important, is Sappho: One Hundred Lyrics, one of the most successful of the numerous attempts which have been made to recapture the poems by that high priestess of song which remain to us only in fragments. Mr. Carman, as Charles G. D. Roberts points out in an introduction to the volume, has made no attempt here at translation or paraphrasing; his venture has been "the most perilous and most alluring in the whole field of poetry"—that of imaginative and, at the same time, interpretive construction. Brief quotation again would fail to convey an adequate idea of the exquisiteness of the work, and all I can do, therefore, is to urge all lovers of real poetry to possess themselves of Sappho: One Hundred Lyrics, for it is literally a storehouse of lyric beauty.

I must not fail here to speak of From the Book of Valentines, which contains some lovely things, notably "At the Great Release." This is not only one of the finest of all Mr. Carman's poems, but it is also one of the finest poems of our time. It is a love poem, and no one possessing any real feeling for poetry can read it without experiencing that strange thrill of the spirit which only the highest form of poetry can communicate. "Morning and Evening," "In an Iris Meadow," and "A letter from Lesbos" must be also mentioned. In the last named poem, Sappho is represented as writing to Gorgo, and expresses herself in these moving words:

If the high gods in that triumphant time
Have calendared no day for thee to come
Light-hearted to this doorway as of old,
Unmoved I shall behold their pomps go by—
The painted seasons in their pageantry,
The silvery progressions of the moon,
And all their infinite ardors unsubdued,
Pass with the wind replenishing the earth

Incredulous forever I must live
And, once thy lover, without joy behold,
The gradual uncounted years go by,
Sharing the bitterness of all things made.

Mention must be now made of Songs of the Sea Children, which can be described only as a collection of the sweetest and tenderest love lyrics written in our time—

—the lyric songs
The earthborn children sing,
When wild-wood laughter throngs
The shy bird-throats of spring;
When there's not a joy of the heart
But flies like a flag unfurled,
And the swelling buds bring back
The April of the world.

So perfect and complete are these lyrics that it would be almost sacrilege to quote any of them unless entire. Listen however, to these verses:

The day is lost without thee,
The night has not a star.
Thy going is an empty room
Whose door is left ajar.

Depart: it is the footfall
Of twilight on the hills.
Return: and every rood of ground
Breaks into daffodils.

There are those who will have it that Bliss Carman has been away from Canada so long that he has ceased to be, in a real sense, a Canadian. Such assume rather than know, for a very little study of his work would show them that it is shot through and through with the poet's feeling for the land of his birth. Memories of his childhood and youthful years down by the sea are still fresh in Mr. Carman's mind, and inspire him again and again in his writing. "A Remembrance," at the beginning of the present collection, may be pointed to as a striking instance of this, but proof positive is the volume, Songs from a Northern Garden, for it could have been written only by a Canadian, born and bred, one whose heart and soul thrill to the thought of Canada. I would single out from this volume for special mention as being "Canadian" in the fullest sense "In a Grand Pré Garden," "The Keeper's Silence," "At Home and Abroad," "Killoleet," and "Above the Gaspereau," but have no space to quote from them.

But Mr. Carman is not only a Canadian, he is also a Briton; and evidence of this is his Ode on the Coronation, written on the occasion of the crowning of King Edward VII in 1902. This poem—the very existence of which is hardly known among us—ought to be put in the hands of every child and youth who speaks the English tongue, for no other, I dare maintain—nothing by Kipling, or Newbolt, or any other of our so-called "Imperial singers"—expresses more truly and more movingly the deep feeling of love and reverence which the very thought of England evokes in every son of hers, even though it may never have been his to see her white cliffs rise or to tread her storied ground:

O England, little mother by the sleepless Northern tide,
Having bred so many nations to devotion, trust, and pride,
Very tenderly we turn
With welling hearts that yearn

Still to love you and defend you,—let the sons of men discern
Wherein your right and title, might and majesty, reside.

In concluding this, I greatly fear, lamentably inadequate study, I come to the collection which follows, and which, as intimated above, represents the work of Mr. Carman's latest period. I must say at once that, while I yield to no one in admiration for Low Tide and the other books of that period, or for the work of the second period, as represented by the Songs from Vagabondia volumes, I have no hesitation in declaring that I regard the poet's work of the past few years with even higher admiration. It may not possess the force and vigor of the work which preceded it; but anything seemingly missing in that respect is more than made up for me by increased beauty and clarity of expression. The mysticism—verging, or more than verging, at times on symbolism—which marked his earlier poems, and which hung, as it were, as a veil between them and the reader, has gone, and the poet's thought or theme now lies clearly before us as in a mirror. What—to take a verse from the following pages at random—could be more pellucid, more crystal clear in expression—what indeed, could come closer to that achieving of the impossible at which every real poet must aim—than this from "In Gold Lacquer".

Gold are the great trees overhead,
And gold the leaf-strewn grass,
As though a cloth of gold were spread
To let a seraph pass.
And where the pageant should go by,
Meadow and wood and stream,
The world is all of lacquered gold,
Expectant as a dream.

The poet, happily, has fully recovered from the serious illness which laid him low some two years ago, and which for a time caused his friends and admirers the gravest concern, and so we may look forward hopefully to seeing further volumes of verse come from the press to make certain his name and fame. But if, for any reason, this should not be—which the gods forfend!—Later Poems, I dare affirm, must and will be regarded as the fine flower and crowning achievement of the genius and art of Bliss Carman.

R. H. HATHAWAY.
Toronto, 1921.

Bliss Carman – A Short Biography

William Bliss Carman was born in Fredericton, in New Brunswick on April 15th 1861. 'Bliss' was his mother's maiden name. She was descended from Daniel Bliss of Concord, Massachusetts, who was the great-grandfather to Ralph Waldo Emerson.

Carman was educated at Fredericton Collegiate School. Here, under the influence of the headmaster George Robert Parkin, he gained an appreciation of classical literature and was introduced to the poetry of many of the Pre-Raphaelites especially Dante Gabriel Rossetti and Algernon Charles Swinburne.

From here he graduated to the University of New Brunswick, obtaining his B.A. there in 1881. As is common with so many writers his first published piece was for the University magazine and for Carman that was in 1879.

England now beckoned and he spent a year at Oxford and then the University of Edinburgh (1882–1883). He returned home to Canada to work on his M.A. which he obtained from the University of New Brunswick in 1884.

Tragically his father died in January, 1885, followed by his mother in February of the following year. Carman now enrolled in Harvard University for a year. There he met and was part of a literary circle that included the American poet Richard Hovey, who would become his close friend, and later collaborator, on the successful Vagabondia poetry series. Carman and Hovey were members of the "Visionists" circle along with Herbert Copeland and F. Holland Day, who would later form the Boston publishing firm Copeland & Day and, in turn, launch Vagabondia.

After Harvard Carman briefly returned to Canada, but was back in Boston by February of 1890 saying "Boston is one of the few places where my critical education and tastes could be of any use to me in earning money. New York and London are about the only other places." However, he was unable to find work in Boston but was more successful in New York becoming the literary editor of the semi-religious New York Independent. There he helped Canadian poets get published and introduced them to a wider readership than they could receive in Canada.

However, Carman and work as an editor were not destined for a long career together and he was dismissed in 1892. There followed short stays with Current Literature, Cosmopolitan, The Chap-Book, and The Atlantic Monthly. Whilst these appointments provided the basis for a career and an income he was not suited to their demands. From 1895 he would only work as a contributor to magazines and newspapers whilst he worked on his volumes of poetry.

Carman first published a book of poetry in 1893 with Low Tide on Grand Pré. He had written the title poem in the summer of 1886 and it had (whilst he was still at Harvard) been published in the spring of 1887 by Atlantic Monthly. Despite its critical acceptance there was no Canadian company prepared to publish the volume. When an American company did so it went bankrupt. Life was becoming difficult for the young poet.

The following year was decidedly better. His partnership with Richard Hovey had given birth to Songs of Vagabondia and it was published by their friends at Copeland & Day. It was an immediate success. The young men were delighted at such a reception. It quickly sold out and was re-printed a number of times. Although these re-prints were small (usually 500-1000 copies) they were frequent.

On the back of this success they would write a further three volumes, which in their turn were almost as successful. They quickly became the center of a cult following, especially among students who empathized with the poetry's anti-materialistic themes, its celebration of personal freedom, and its glorification of comradeship."

The success of Songs of Vagabondia prompted the Boston firm, Stone & Kimball, to reissue Low Tide on Grand Pré and to hire Carman as the editor of its literary journal, The Chapbook. This ceased after a year when the company relocated and Carman expressed his desire to remain in Boston.

In 1885 Carman brought out Behind the Arras, a somewhat more serious and philosophical work centered on the premise of a long meditation using the speaker's house and its many rooms as a symbol of life and the choices to be made. However, the idea and its execution did not quite meld.

Signficantly, in 1896, Carman met Mrs Mary Perry King, who rapidly became patron, adviser and sometime lover. She put money in his pocket, and food in his mouth and, when he struck bottom, often repaired his confidence as well as helping to sell the work. She also later became his writing collaborator on two verse dramas.

Mitchell Kennerley, Carman's roommate wrote that, "On the rare occasions they had intimate relations they always advised me of by leaving a bunch of violets — Mary favorite flower — on the pillow of my bed." If her husband, Dr. King, knew of this arrangement he seems not to have objected. He was a great supporter of Carman's career and seemingly his wife's complicated involvement with that.

In 1897 Carman published Ballad of Lost Haven, a collection of poetry about the sea. Its notable poems include the macabre sea shanty, The Gravedigger. The following year, 1898, came By the Aurelian Wall, the title poem itself was an elegy to John Keats and the book a collection of formal elegies.

In 1899 his publisher, Lamson, Wolffe was taken over by the Boston firm of Small, Maynard & Co., who had also acquired the rights to Low Tide on Grand Pré. The copyrights to of his books were now held by one publisher and, in lieu of earnings, Carman took what would ultimately be a disastrous financial stake in the company.

As the century turned Carman was hard at work on what would eventually be a five-volume set of poetry; "Pans Pipes". Pan, the goat-god, was traditionally associated with poetry and the coming together of the earthly and the divine. The five volumes were all published between 1902 – 1905.

The inspiration for this came from Mary who had persuaded Carman to write in both prose and poetry about the ideas of 'unitrinianism.' This drew on the theories of François-Alexandre-Nicolas-Chéri Delsarte and was defined as a strategy of mind-body-spirit harmonization aimed at undoing the physical, psychological, and spiritual damage caused by urban modernity. The definition may be rather woolly but for Carman it resulted in some very fine work across the five-volume series. This shared belief between Mary and Carman created a further bond but did isolate him from his circle of friends.

The excellence of a number of these poems did much to install Carman as the most noted of Canadian Poets and eventually their own Poet Laureate. Among the most often quoted and printed are "The Dead Faun" (from Volume I), "Lord of My Heart's Elation" (Volume II) and many of the erotic poems from Volume III.

In the middle of publication in 1903, Small, Maynard failed and with it went all the assets Carman had tied up in the company.

Carman immediately signed with another Boston publisher, L.C. Page, who would publish seven new books of Carman poetry in this hectic period up to 1905. They released a further three books based on Carman's Transcript columns, and a prose work on Unitrinianism, The Making of Personality, that he'd written with Mary King.

Carman now felt secure enough to pursue his 'dream project,' namely a deluxe edition of his collected poetry to 1903. Page acquired the distribution rights on the condition that the book be sold privately, by subscription. Unfortunately, the demand wasn't there and it failed. Carman was deeply disappointed and lost faith in Page. However, their grip on his copyrights was absolute and sadly no further collected editions were to be published during his lifetime.

By 1904 his income was restricted and the offer to be editor-in-chief of the 10-volume project, The World's Best Poetry, was eagerly accepted.

For Carman perhaps his best years as a poet were now behind him. From 1908 he lived near the Kings' New Canaan, Connecticut, estate, that he named "Sunshine", or in the summer in a cabin in the Catskills, which he called "Moonshine."

With Literary tastes now moving away from what he could provide his income further dwindled and his health started to deteriorate.

In 1912 Carman published the final work in the Vagabondia series. Richard Hovey had died in 1900 and so this last work was purely his. It has a distinct elegiac tone as if remembering the past works themselves.

Although Carman was not politically active he did campaign during the World War One, as a member of the Vigilantes, who supported the American entry into the titanic struggle on the Allied side.

By 1920, Carman was impoverished and recovering from a near-fatal attack of tuberculosis. He returned to Canada and began to undertake a series of publicly successful and somewhat lucrative reading tours, saying "there is nothing worth talking of in book sales compared with reading. Breathless attention, crowded halls, and a strange, profound enthusiasm such as I never guessed could be,' he reported to a friend. 'And good thrifty money too. Think of it! An entirely new life for me, and I am the most surprised person in Canada.'"

On October 28th, 1921 Carman was honored at a dinner held by the newly-formed Canadian Authors' Association, at the Ritz Carlton Hotel in Montreal, where he was crowned Canada's Poet Laureate with a wreath of maple leaves.

Carman is placed among the Confederation Poets, a group that included his cousin, Charles G.D. Roberts, Archibald Lampman, and Duncan Campbell Scott. Carman was perhaps the best and is credited with the widest recognition. However, whilst the others carefully supplemented their income with writing novels and works for the magazines, or even other careers, Carman only wrote poetry together with a small amount of writing on literary ideas, philosophy, and aesthetics.

He continued his reading tours, and by 1925 had finally secured a new Canadian publisher; McClelland & Stewart (Toronto), who issued a collection of selected earlier verse and would now became his main publisher. Although they benefited from Carman's increased popularity and his revered position in Canadian literature, his former publisher L.C. Page would not relinquish its copyrights to his earlier works.

In his last years, Carman was a member of the Halifax literary and social set, The Song Fishermen and in 1927 he edited The Oxford Book of American Verse.

William Bliss Carman died of a brain hemorrhage, at the age of 68, in New Canaan on the 8th June, 1929. He was cremated in New Canaan and his ashes interred at Forest Hill Cemetery, Fredericton, with a national memorial service held at the Anglican cathedral there.

It was only a quarter of a century later, on May 13th, 1954, that a scarlet maple tree was planted at his graveside, to honour his request in the 1892 poem "The Grave-Tree":

Let me have a scarlet maple
For the grave-tree at my head,
With the quiet sun behind it,
In the years when I am dead.

Bliss Carman – A Concise Bibliography

Poetry Collections
Low Tide on Grand Pre: A Book of Lyrics (1893)
Songs from Vagabondia (1894)
A Seamark: A Threnody for Robert Louis Stevenson (1895)
Behind the Arras: A Book of the Unseen (1895)
More Songs from Vagabondia (1896)
Ballads of Lost Haven: A Book of the Sea (1897)
By the Aurelian Wall: And Other Elegies (1898)
A Winter Holiday (1899)
Last Songs from Vagabondia (1901)
Ballads and Lyrics (1902)
Ode on the Coronation of King Edward (1902)
Pipes of Pan: From the Book of Myths (1902)
Pipes of Pan: From the Green Book of the Bards (1903)
Pipes of Pan: Songs of the Sea Children (1904)
Pipes of Pan: Songs from a Northern Garden (1904)
Pipes of Pan: From the Book of Valentines (1905)
Sappho: One Hundred Lyrics (1904)
Poems (1905)
The Rough Rider: And Other Poems (1909)
A Painter's Holiday, and Other Poems (1911)
Echoes from Vagabondia (1912)
April Airs: A Book of New England Lyrics (1916)
The Man of The Marne: And Other Poems (1918)
The Vengeance of Noel Brassard: A Tale of the Acadian Expulsion (1919)
Far Horizons (1925)
Later Poems (1926)
Sanctuary: Sunshine House Sonnets (1929)
Wild Garden (1929)
Bliss Carman's Poems (1931)

Drama
Bliss Carman & Mary Perry King. Daughters of Dawn: A Lyrical Pageant of a Series of Historical Scenes for Presentation with Music and Dancing (1913)
Bliss Carman & Mary Perry King. Earth Deities: And Other Rhythmic Masques (1914)

Prose Collections
The Kinship of Nature (1904)
The Poetry of Life (1905)
The Friendship of Art (1908)
The Making of Personality (1908)
Talks on Poetry and Life; Being a Series of Five Lectures Delivered Before the University of Toronto, December 1925 (Speech). transcribed by Blanche Hume. 1926.
Bliss Carman's Scrap-Book: A Table of Contents (Pierce, Lorne, editor) (1931)

Editor
The World's Best Poetry (10 volumes) (1904)
The Oxford Book of American Verse (U.S. editor) (1927)
Carman, Bliss; Pierce, Lorne, editors (1935). Our Canadian Literature: Representative Verse, English and French.

www.ingramcontent.com/pod-product-compliance
Lightning Source LLC
Chambersburg PA
CBHW060053050426
42448CB00011B/2439